CONTENTS

Bristlecone Pine:
The oldest known living thing.

THE AUTHOR: Len Ettinger is a registered geologist and licensed attorney who has spent many years traveling the western United States. He is also author of *The Rockhound and Prospector's Bible.*

ISBN-10: 1500251593
ISBN-13: 978-1500251598
Cover—Dan Heath
Typesetting/Layout—Ann Callahan-Ettinger
Copyright ©1989 by L.J. Ettinger
All Rights Reserved

Published by Len Ettinger
Executive publisher Vicki L. Tam

ljettinger.com

Printed in the U.S.A.

INTRODUCTION

Once upon a time .... Our Earth formed about 4.6 billion years ago and has since then gone through many changes. Rocks along U.S. 395 tell a story about the collision of crustal plates, mountain building, faulting, volcanos, and glacial periods. This Travel Guide will help you understand that story.

U.S. 395, California 14 and 1-5 cut across 468 miles of mountains, valleys, and desert between Reno and Los Angeles. The route is rich in scenic beauty, geology and history.

Traveling south from Reno, U.S. 395 and State 14 generally follow the eastern boundary of the Sierra Nevada and western edge of the Basin and Range Province, cut across the northwest corner of the Mojave Desert, cross the San Andreas Fault, then traverse the northern San Gabriel Mountains and into the Los Angeles Basin. Igneous, sedimentary, and metamorphic rocks, ranging in age from Precambrian to Recent, are found along the way.

There is also another story: the story of man in the western United States. Imagine a barren land, a land without roads, without cities or towns, and few signs of civilization. Man's adventures in the western United States began over 10,000 years ago with the Indians, followed by the Spanish some 400 years ago.

Imagine Paiute Indians, their villages, their hunting parties. Imagine explorers and prospectors, wagon trains, emigrants and settlers. Pioneers started westward in the 1840s, and were fol-lowed by thousands during the gold rushes of 1849 to the Mother Lode in California, and 1859 to the Comstock Lode in Nevada.

Imagine Model T Fords on rutted dirt roads. Imagine battles for water rights between the City of Los Angeles and settlers of the Owens Valley. The 1920-1930 period saw the west criss-crossed with new roads to accommodate auto travel, followed by interstate highways of the 1960s and 70s.

This Travel Guide should make your auto trip a little more fun and educational by directing your attention to geological features and historical points of interest along the route.

Use this Travel Guide as written when traveling from Reno to Los Angeles, and reverse the order when traveling from Los Angeles to Reno.

Locations are described using mile markers — seen as small lettered and numbered posts along the highway. Letters refer to the county and numbers are the miles from the county line.

Happy traveling,

Len Ettinger

January, 1989

1

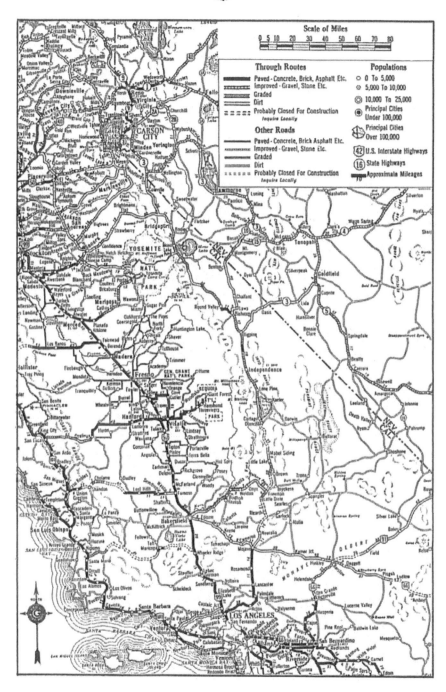

Early 1930s Firestone official road map of California and Nevada. Note that a little over 100 miles of road between Reno and Los Angeles were paved.

TRAVELING FROM RENO TO LOS ANGELES

Wa 25. **RENO**—Pop. 100,756 (1980), El. 4,450'. "Biggest Little City in the World." The first whites passed through the area with the Stevens-Murphy emigrant party in 1844 and settlement began in the early 1850s. Charles Fuller established a river ferry across the Truckee in the fall of 1859 and completed a bridge and hotel in the spring of 1860. Myron C. Lake acquired Fuller's holdings in 1861, rebuilt the bridge and established Lake's Crossing. In 1868, Lake offered land for a depot to the Central Pacific Railroad and the town was laid out. Named in honor of General Jesse Lee Reno, a federal officer who died in the Civil War.

Growth was rapid due to railroad activity and continued development of the nearby Comstock mines. Reno became the Washoe County seat in 1871, incorporated in 1876, but did not draw up a charter or hold elections until 1903.

In 1906 the wife of a prominent United States industrialist came to Reno for a divorce. The resulting publicity started the city's divorce reputation. On July 4, 1910, Reno hosted "The Fight of the Century" between Jack Johnson, the black heavyweight champion, and ex-champion Jim Jeffries, "The Great White Hope." Some 22,000 saw Johnson win as Jeffries' trainers threw in the towel in the 15th round. Tourism increased, and a new industry was established when gambling was legalized in 1931.

Wa 16-15. **STEAMBOAT SPRINGS**—One of the largest geothermal fumarole fields in the United States. Hot springs and fumaroles vent water ranging from 360 to 450°F at depth. Named by early emigrants because of their puffing and blowing, Steamboat was settled in 1860 by Felix Monet. In 1861 a hospital and adjacent bath-houses were constructed.

As a result of the Comstock mining activities, in 1871 Steamboat became a terminal for the Virginia and Truckee Railroad. Materials for the silver mines were transferred to freight wagons for the steep haul to Virginia City along Old Geiger Grade Toll Road. Completion of the rail line negated the need for a station. During the bonanza period, Steamboat had a fine hotel with dance hall and elegant bar to which came the legendary silver kings, politicians, gamblers and news chroniclers.

Today, because of a lack of foresight by federal, state, and local governmental officials to protect this unique landmark, Steamboat Springs is a hodge podge of private and federal land, with two geothermal power plants which, starting in 1986, produce approximately 20 MW of power.

The **COMSTOCK LODE** and **VIRGINIA CITY**—After Mormon pioneers, at Brigham Young's orders in 1849, settled the Carson, Eagle and Washoe valleys, placer gold was discovered at the mouth of Six Mile Canyon near Dayton. It took 10 years for the placer miners to work their way six miles up the mountain where the Comstock Lode was discovered. Virginia City was established and $350 million in gold and silver was mined during the next 20 years. The Comstock Lode is one of the most famous mining districts in the world and its discovery played an important role in the development of Reno, Carson City and Washoe Valley due to the need for supplies, lumber and water to work the mines.

VIRGINIA AND TRUCKEE RAILROAD—Constructed during 1869-1872 connecting Reno and Virginia City through Carson City. The first train traversed the 52-mile route on September 1, 1872, and the last steamed on May 31, 1950. Remains of the rail bed can be seen occasionally through Washoe Valley.

WASHOE VALLEY AND LAKE—Named after the Washoe Indians, a peaceful people who hunted and fished and still celebrate their pine-nut ceremony annually. The communities of Washoe City and Franktown developed in the Washoe Valley to process Comstock ore at large stamp mills, and also to store great quantities of timber that would be shipped to the mines.

Wa 0 (CC 7). Lakeview—In 1863 there were two hotels (and stables), one of which became a station for the Virginia and Truckee Railroad in 1872. Three inverted siphon pipelines crossing under the highway, furnished water along a 67-mile box flume and pipeline system from the Sierra Nevada watershed to Virginia City from 1873 to the present.

In 1881, Lakeview became a lumber storage area for timber cut in the Lake Tahoe Basin, reaching a peak in 1887 as lumber was fed to the yard by a V-flume originating above Incline Village. Timber products were shipped to the Comstock mines by rail until 1896.

EAGLE VALLEY—Site of Carson City, and Carson branch of the California Emigrant Trail, which crossed the Sierra at Kit Carson Pass.

4

CC 5. **FIRST AIR FLIGHT IN NEVADA**—June 23, 1910, just west of the highway. Ivy Baldwin, a nationally known parachutist and balloonist, made the flight in a 48-horsepower Curtis Paullan biplane, reaching an altitude of 50 feet and covering a one-half mile loop. At the time this was the highest altitude (4,675 feet) ever reached.

CC 4-2. **CARSON CITY**—Pop. 32,022 (1980), El. 4,665'. Capital of Nevada, and one of the state's oldest towns, it was first established in 1851 as Eagle Station, a trading post and small ranch on the Carson branch of the California Emigrant Trail kept by Frank and W.L. Hall and George Jollenshee. The station and surrounding valley took their names from an eagle skin stretched on the trading post wall.

From 1855 to 1857, Mormon colonizers under Elder Orson Hyde settled in Eagle, Carson and Washoe valleys. In 1857, they were called back to Salt Lake City by Brigham Young.

Carson City itself was founded and laid out in 1858 by Abraham Curry, who bought the Eagle Station and ranch when he found lots at Genoa too expensive. Curry named this town after the Carson River which was named after famed explorer Kit Carson, and left a plaza in its center for his predicted location of the state capital.

A view of the principal street in Carson City, late 1800s.

5

In the 1860s, Carson City was a station on the Pony Express and the Overland mail routes. In 1861, true to Curry's prediction and aided considerably by his own shrewd maneuvers, Carson City became the capital of Nevada Territory. When Nevada became a state in 1864, Carson City was the state's capital, and in 1870 the present capitol building was completed in the plaza Curry had reserved for it.

Most of the early state and federal buildings were constructed of sandstone blocks quarried near the state prison a few miles to the east.

CC 2. Gardner's Ranch—From 1870 to 1918, the Gardner Ranch covered 300 acres of meadowland. Matthew Gardner also logged south of Lake Tahoe for the Carson-Tahoe Lumber and Fluming Company, which was the greatest of the Comstock lumbering operations between 1870-1898. The immense lumberyard was approximately one mile long and one-half mile wide at the terminus of a 12-mile long "V" flume from Spooner Summit in the Sierra Nevada.

CARSON VALLEY—A broad expanse of cultivated pastureland south of Carson City was originally a strip of meadow along the banks of the Carson River where 49ers followed the California branch of the emigrant trail, rested their stock and bought vegetables from the Mormon settlers. In 1850 the first settlement was established at Mormon Station, renamed Genoa in 1856, which became a center for British settlers. In 1861, Nevada's territorial government was established at Genoa.

Pony Express riders used this route in 1860, switching in 1861 to the shorter Daggett Trail (Kingsbury Grade). In 1861 Utah Territory granted franchises for the construction of the Cradlebaugh and Boyd toll roads linking Carson City, Genoa and the Aurora mining camp. Twelve Mile House was built at the intersection of these two toll roads and still stands.

Starting in 1898, Spanish and French Basque shepherds tended some 13,000 sheep in the Carson Valley, increasing to 25,000 by 1925, when the Basques began acquiring their own sheep and land.

Fault scarps along the base of the Sierra to the west are evidence of recent major earthquakes in a seismically active zone extending north to Reno. Walley's Hot Springs, two miles south of Genoa, Carson Hot Springs, and Steamboat Springs are all within this zone.

Do 23. Minden—El. 4,720'. Established in 1905 by H.F. Dangberg (Land and Livestock Co.) as a station for the Virginia and Truckee Railroad. Named after the town in Germany where Dangberg was born.

Do 21-20. Gardnerville—Pop. 2,638 (1980), El. 4,750'. Named for area rancher, John Gardner. Early Gardnerville served the farming community and teamsters hauling local produce to the booming mining camp of Bodie. The first buildings were a blacksmith shop, saloon and hotel. Gardnerville became a center for Danish immigrants in 1870.

Do 18. Dresslerville—In 1917 State Senator William Dressler gave a 40-acre tract to the Washoe Indians, then living on ranches in the Carson Valley. In 1924, it became the nucleus of a Washoe settlement.

CALIFORNIA STATE LINE—*Rest Area.*

Topaz Lake. Dam built in 1912.

Mono 115. Topaz—Pop. 100, El. 5,040'. Established in 1885. Named after the mineral topaz which is found in nearby hills.

Mono 111. Coleville—Pop. 43, El. 5,160'. Named after Cornelius Cole, California congressman, 1863-1867.

Mono 108-107. Walker—Pop. 300, El. 5,400'.

Mono 90. Fales Hot Springs—Fossil hot springs aprons in road cut. Water temperatures range from 140-150°F. First seen during the second Fremont expedition on January 27, 1844, and developed by Sam Fales in 1877, who patented 160 acres of land surrounding the springs in 1882.

Mono 88. Devil's Gate Pass—El. 7,519'.

Mono 76. **BRIDGEPORT**—Pop. 300, El. 6,465'. Settled in late 1850s as Big Meadows. Established in 1864 as Mono County seat and named Bridgeport because of proximity to footbridge across the East Walker River. Numerous hot springs east of town.

Mono 69. Dogtown Historic Marker—Gold was discovered in 1857 and placer mined in gulch to the west until 1859.

Cutoff to the ghost mining town of Bodie, 13 miles east of U.S. 395. Bodie has been a California State Park since 1962.

BODIE—One of the last of California's old-time mining camps. Gold was discovered near Bodie in late 1859 by William S. Bodey. The name Bodie, resulting from a misspelled sign, was given to the small mining camp that sprang up after the discovery. The real stampede came in 1877 with additional discoveries in the area. Many who arrived came from the declining Comstock Lode.

Eight thousand resided in Bodie in 1879, a town with a reputation for violence and toughness, where shootings, stabbings, and thefts took place nearly every day. By November 1881, the population dropped below 3,000 and by 1887, only 1,500 remained. Production continued until the early 1900s, totalling $50-$60 million. By 1921 only 30 residents remained. The great fire of 1932 destroyed most of the town.

Mono 63. Conway Summit—El. 8,138'. Named after John Conway who settled the area in 1880. Glacial deposits overlie granite in road cuts.

Mono 61. Typical granite outcrops.

Mono 58-57. Highway cuts through glacial moraine.

MONO LAKE—A saline remnant of a vast inland sea that covered approximately 316 square miles of the Mono Basin and Aurora Valley more than 13,000 years ago. Since retreat of the glaciers the lake has shrunk to approximately 85 square miles and its level has fluctuated plus or minus 100 feet.

Named by the Yokut Indians for the Shoshonean Indians who lived along the shores (means fly-people because their wealth and main source of food were the countless millions of the pupae of a fly). Early explorers called Mono Lake the "Dead Sea of the West."

Mono Lake water is transported to southern California through the Los Angeles aqueduct. Since 1941, when the Mono aqueduct extension began operation the lake level has dropped one foot per year. This increased to 1.6 feet per year with the second aqueduct in 1970. There is an ongoing legal battle between environmentalists and the City of Los Angeles to halt the dropping lake level and even to raise it for environmental purposes, including preservation of gull nesting grounds and tiny brine shrimp, flies and infusoria, necessary for the life balance in the area.

Mono 50-51. Lee Vining—Pop. 315, El. 6,780'. Named for Leroy Vining, who settled in the area and operated a saw mill in the 1850s. Gateway to Yosemite via Tioga Pass to the west.

Mono Lake by J. Ross Browne, 1865.

INYO AND MONO CRATERS—Explosive volcanic activity has occurred in the region for some three million years. Between Mono Lake and Mammoth at least 20 eruptions have occurred in the last 2,000 years. Boiling springs and steam vents abound and evidence suggests that magma presently exists about six miles beneath the surface of Mono Craters. Panum Crater is dated at 640 years.

Mono 39-35. Mono Craters—Consists of 20 volcanic domes rising about 2,600 feet above surrounding plains, east of the highway.

Mono 38. Wilson Butte—Rhyolite dome along west side of road.

Mono 35. Deadman Summit. El. 8,036'.

Mono 32. *Rest Stop.* Entering northwest part of Long Valley Caldera.

Mono 26. Mammoth Lakes. Pop. 3,929 (1980)—In June 1877,

U.S. GEOLOGICAL SURVEY

W.D. Johnson, Topographer

EIGHTH ANNUAL REPORT PL. XL, 1888

I.C. Russell, Geologist.

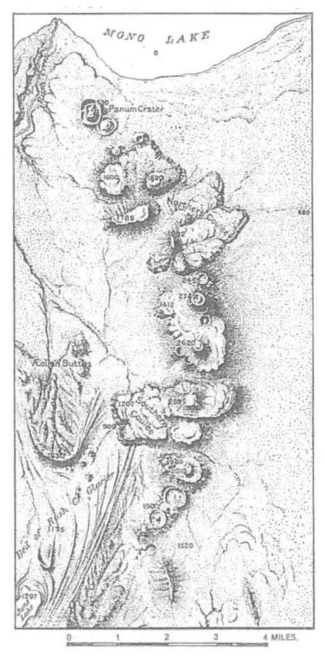

Elevation above Lake Mono given in feet
MONO CRATERS

four men located gold at an elevation of 11,000 feet. A mining district was formed and the Mammoth Mining Company began work in 1878. The town had a post office from 1879-1881, and again from 1896 to 1898. Total production of gold and silver was about $1 million. Now a popular winter and summer resort area.

LONG VALLEY CALDERA—Long Valley is an ancient caldera, a fault-bounded elliptical basin whose floor sank to a depth of one-half mile or more below sea level about 700,000 years ago. It sank during catastrophic eruption which emptied its magma chamber of about 150 cubic miles of fine ash (identified as far east as Nebraska), pumice, and a frothy mixture of ash and pumice that cooled and hardened as the Bishop Tuff (reddish, porous rock that blankets the area — best seen south of Crowley Lake and down the grade toward Bishop).

Between 1979 and 1982, swarms of earthquakes occurred in the Mammoth area indicating magma had risen from a depth of 4.2 miles to 2.1 miles and led to a USGS Stage I volcanic eruption alert. When earthquake activity subsided in 1982, the alert was cancelled.

Mono 21. **CONVICT LAKE**—Glacial lake two miles west of highway.

Twenty-nine convicts including murderers, rapists, train robbers and horse thieves, escaped from the Nevada State Penitentiary at Carson City on September 17, 1871. Six of them headed south and murdered a mail rider from Aurora. Posses from Aurora and Benton caught up to the convicts near "Monte Diablo Creek," now Convict Creek. A Benton merchant, who was leading the posse, was killed in the encounter. The convicts escaped, but three of them were captured a few days later and two were lynched while being returned to Carson City.

Mono 19-14. **CROWLEY LAKE**—An artificial reservoir behind a 167-foot dam completed in 1941 by the City of Los Angeles at the southern end of Long Valley. Named after Father John Crowley, Owens Valley's first resident priest who played an important role in improving relations between the City of Los Angeles and Owens Valley residents during the water battles of the 1930s.

Mono 8. Sherwin Summit—El. 7,000'. Named for James Sherwin who had a ranch at the base of the hill and who, in 1877, built the Sherwin Toll Road up the grade during the gold rush to the Mammoth Mines.

Note glacial moraine where canyons empty into valleys along the Sierra front.

SIERRA NEVADA BATHOLITH—The Sierra Nevada batholith originated during the Nevadan phase of the Cordilleran Orogeny (195-80 million years ago) as the result of hundreds of intrusions over an area 75 miles wide and trending in a north-south direction the length of California.

The driving force was created by the impact of the southwest-moving North American crustal plate with that of the northwest-moving Kula plate. The Kula plate was forced under the North American plate forming an east dipping subduction zone from which arose great teardrop-shaped masses of magma (See Geologic Cross Sections). The magma reached equilibrium with the surrounding crustal rocks at depths estimated at two to five miles, and cooled as granites and granodiorites, below a surface being uplifted to Andean heights (15,000 to 20,000'). The present Sierra are the result of subsequent uplift, faulting and erosion.

GLACIERS—During the ice ages of the last one million years, accumulations of snow formed piles thousands of feet thick in the high Sierra canyons, which were pressured into ice. Under the force of gravity, the ice began to flow slowly down the flanks of the mountains as glaciers, ripping the rocks and turning V-shaped canyons into U-shaped valleys. When the glaciers melted during warmer times, great deposits of rock material scraped from the canyons were left as moraines in the valleys. Today some 50 active glaciers are found in the high Sierra. By far the largest is the Palisade Glacier which drains into Big Pine Creek.

Inyo 116-115. **BISHOP**—Pop. 3,333 (1980), El. 4,147'. Established in 1864, when a saw mill was built to serve nearby mines. Named for Samuel Bishop, a local cattleman who came to California in 1849 and, in 1861, camped in the Owens Valley along Bishop Creek, three miles southwest of Bishop. Originally called Bishop Creek or Upper Town.

Bishop property, long unsurveyed, was bought and sold by measured metes and bounds for years; in some instances lot descriptions began with such starting points as "a willow tree," "the center of a ditch," etc. This made trouble later when exact boundaries became important.

In the 1880s and 90s Bishop was served by the Carson and Colorado narrow gauge railroad which stopped at Laws, about five miles northeast of Bishop. The railroad museum at Laws is one of the best in the West.

Incorporation of Bishop was voted 63 to 36 on April 24, 1903, and continued to grow serving farming, cattle and dairy industries of the Owens Valley until 1926, when the valley's water was diverted to Los Angeles. Bishop is the only incorporated city in Inyo and Mono counties.

OWENS VALLEY—About 80 miles long and two to five miles wide, the Owens Valley is bounded on the west by the Sierra (Mt. Whitney, El. 14,495'), and on the east by the Inyo-White Mountains (White Mountain Peak, El. 14,246'). Uplifting of the Sierra and Inyo-White Mountains, and down-dropping of the Owens Valley began some three million years ago, with significant movement in the last 700,000 years. Valley fill in the Lone Pine area is about 8,000 feet, which places granite bedrock some 4,000 feet below sea level. Movement is still very active.

Inyo 109. Grand Army of the Republic Highway—Named after a society of men who fought for the North in the Civil War.

Inyo 104. Cal Tech's Radio Observatory ("Big Ears")—Two 90-foot and one 130-foot dish antennae. Part of a global network probing the heavens. Utilizing radio waves, astronomers can see farther than with the largest optical telescope. This site was selected because high mountains on both sides screen out interfering radio and television waves.

Inyo 101-99. Big Pine—Pop. 1,510 (1980), El. 4,000'. Named for a group of unusually large pine trees one-half mile southwest of town. Established in the mid-1860s to support a sawmill built on Big Pine Creek, which operated for many years supplying nearby towns and mines as far away as Cerro Gordo. Approximately 23 miles northeast of Big Pine in the White Mountains is the Ancient Bristlecone Pine Forest, with the world's oldest living trees (Methuselah has been dated at 4,600 years).

Inyo 99-82. **BIG PINE VOLCANIC FIELD**—Includes about 10 cinder cones extending from the base of the Sierra across the

13

Owens Valley to the Inyo Mountains front. These cinder cones and basalt flows range in age from 10,000 to 100,000 years.

The Big Pine volcanic field and the Little Lake field to the south are different in nature from the Mono-Mammoth field north of Bishop. Whereas the Mono-Mammoth field is composed of rhyolitic and rhyodacitic volcanics (the extrusive equivalents of granites of the Sierra Nevada batholith), the Big Pine and Little Lake fields consist of basalts and are related to the severe basin and range faulting bounding the Sierra and Inyo Mountains, which acted as deep crustal conduits for the basaltic lavas.

Inyo 84. *Rest Area.*

BASIN AND RANGE—U.S. 395 follows the approximate boundary between the Sierra Nevada to the west and the Basin and Range Province to the east. About 17 million years ago most of the present Basin and Range was a low lying volcanic plain. Triggered by upwelling heat from the upper mantle, uplift of thousands of feet began, resulting in thinning of the crust and faulted uplift of mountains and downdropping of basins (see Geologic Cross Sections). About seven million years ago, sediments derived from erosion of the mountains began flooding the valleys, some to depths of 10,000 feet. Areas of the basin and range are seismically active today.

Inyo 76. Camp Independence cutoff—Established July 4, 1862, to protect miners and settlers from the Paiute Indians. The camp was active between 1862-1863 and 1865-1877. After the 1872 earthquake the camp was rebuilt with officers' housing, a hospital, school, store rooms and a commissary, all painted white and surrounding a parade ground. Since 1902, a portion of the military reserve was set aside for use by the Paiute Indian population, which numbered 811 in 1930.

Inyo 73. Independence—Pop. 1,000, El. 3,925'. Established in 1866 and named for Camp Independence. Originally settled in 1861 as Putnam's, then as Little Pine. Fire destroyed most of central Independence on June 30, 1886 because no fire fighting apparatus was available.

LOS ANGELES AND OWENS VALLEY WATER

Owens Valley was occupied by the Paiute Indians before the white settlers arrived. White trappers and explorers passed through the Owens Valley as early as 1833 and in 1859 a military column led by Captain J.W. Davidson, entered the valley. His report included passages such as "Every step now taken shows you that nature has been lavish of her stores.... The mountains are filled with timber, the valley's (sic) with water and meadows of luxuriant (sic) grass. Some of these meadows contain, at a moderate estimate, ten thousand acres, every foot of which can be irrigated.... Wherever water touches it, it produces abundantly. I should think it well suited to the growth of wheat, barley, oats, rye and various fruits, the apple, pear, etc. . . . . . To the Graziers, this is one of the finest parts of the State; to the Farmer, it offers every advantage but a market." Davidson's glowing report attracted the attention of white settlers, miners, and cattlemen, who began arriving in increasing numbers in the early 1860s.

In the 1860s, large herds of cattle were driven into the valley for winter range and small farms began to spring up. The white man's invasion of the Owens Valley caused a disruption of the Indian way of life and resulted in numerous altercations. By 1899 there were a total of 424 farms in operation on 141,059 acres of the valley, almost all owned by families who lived and worked on plots of 175 acres or less.

Development of the valley's potential was only waiting for adequate transportation facilities to carry its products to a major metropolitan market.

The idea of bringing Owens Valley water to Los Angeles entirely by gravity flow was first proposed in 1885. A real-life drama followed. The players were Fred Eton, who promoted the idea in the 1890s; William Mulholland (1855-1935), Superintendent of the Los Angeles Water Co.; the federal government; departments of the Interior and Reclamation; the State of California; the City of Los Angeles; and the residents of Inyo and Mono counties. Also included were the Los Angeles "Elite": a group of self-serving greedy businessmen including Harrison Gray Otis, publisher of the *Los Angeles Times* and owner of the *Los Angeles Herald*; Harry Chandler, Otis' son-in-law and Los Angeles land developer; E.H. Harriman, president of the Southern Pacific Railroad; Moses Sherman, member of the Los

Angeles Board of Water Commissioners; Henry Huntington, founder of the Pacific Electric Railway Co. in 1901; and W.G. Kerckhoff, president of Pacific Light and Power Co. All of these individuals were part of a San Fernando land syndicate which in 1905 needed Owens Valley water at any cost to develop their land interests.

Through all levels of politics and political means, including lies, deceptions, bribes and misstatements, the Owens Valley aqueduct project was approved by the Los Angeles Water Commission on May 22, 1905. In its original form, it included a 233-mile aqueduct, 142 tunnels totaling 53 miles, 60 miles of open canal, .97 miles of concrete conduit, 12 miles of steel siphons, 120 miles of railroad track, 500 miles of highways and trails, two small power plants to service construction work, 169 miles of transmission lines and 240 miles of telephone wire.

The Los Angeles aqueduct project at that time (1907) was the fourth largest engineering project in American history, surpassed in scope and complexity only by the building of the Panama Canal, the New York Aqueduct and the Erie Canal. Tunneling began on September 20, 1907, and the first water arrived in San Fernando on November 5, 1913, at a cost of $24.5 million for an aqueduct capable of transporting 456 cubic feet per second.

The Mono Extension was started in 1934 and completed in late 1940. It included an 11.3-mile tunnel through craters of extinct volcanos, which encountered steam, hot water and volcanic gases. Water is stored in Crowley Reservoir and funnelled through hydrogenerators for power in a 3,000-foot drop to the Owens Valley.

The second aqueduct was started in August 1964 and was completed in 1970, delivering 210 cubic feet per second at a cost of $100 million.

The first armed conflicts in the Owens Valley were in the 1920s. In 1924, Owens Valley ranchers and residents began blowing up sections of the aqueduct and on November 16 ranchers seized the Alabama Gates, which controlled the main flow of water into the aqueduct. The matter was settled on November 29th.

In 1931 the Los Angeles Department of Water and Power began buying up lots in Bishop, Laws, Big Pine, Independence and Lone Pine, ultimately spending $11 million. By 1933 Los Angeles owned 95 percent of all private farmlands and 85

16

percent of the town properties in the Owens Valley.

In Bishop, Los Angeles kept one-fourth of the town's total land area and one-third of its taxable lands as vacant lots rented for grazing horses and sheep.

In order to better relations between Los Angeles and the residents of the Owens Valley, with Father Crowley acting as an unofficial mediator, the Department of Water and Power began selling town properties back to private citizens in 1939 and by 1944 had disposed of nearly 50 percent of all the town properties Los Angeles had acquired.

Father Crowley's untimely death in 1940, and renewed bitterness between Los Angeles water development policies and Owens Valley residents, resulted in Los Angeles halting all land sales in the valley in March 1945. Even as late as 1966 the City of Bishop did not impose any zoning restrictions of its own, leaving land use regulations to the Los Angeles Department of Water and Power.

Los Angeles could not have grown and developed without Owens Valley water. Between 1914 and 1923 most of the San Fernando Valley and areas of west Los Angeles were annexed by the City of Los Angeles, which increased from 108 to more than 350 square miles.

Today the City of Los Angeles owns about 235,000 acres in Inyo County and 65,000 acres in Mono County. The battle for water rights, which ultimately led to the collapse of the Owens Valley economy and subsequent devastation of local agriculture, snuffed out the development of thousands of acres of farm and orchard land in the Owens Valley and involved the courts, elections, armed night riders, repeated bombing of the aqueduct and truck loads of armed security guards.

Private greed combined with municipal ambition caused needless ruin of one of the most attractive homelands of the west. It was unbelievable that such a valley could revert to primitive waste.

The second major battle began in 1972 in the courts and is on going with no clear winners. Ultimately, it is in everyone's best interest for the City of Los Angeles to come to some kind of just settlement with Owens Valley residents.

Inyo 70. **MOUNT WHITNEY**—El. 14,495'. Highest point in the continental United States. Exploring the Sierra in July 1864, a state geological survey party was astounded to find several peaks higher than Mount Shasta, considered at that time the highest mountain in the west (14,162'). Named by Clarence King after the survey's chief and eminent geologist, Josiah D. Whitney. In 1873, it was found that the peak King named was not the highest peak, and the true Mount Whitney lay several miles to the north.

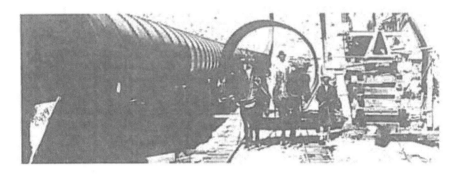

Construction of the Los Angeles aqueduct. The track was constructed parallel to the siphon and mules pulled each section up the mountain.

Inyo 67. **MANZANAR**—In 1909, as a land promotion scheme, a small community was built including a packing house, general store, blacksmith shop, school, lumber yard and ice cream parlor. More than 500 acres were planted in apples, pears, peaches, plums, and grapes. Los Angeles subsequently obtained the water rights which doomed the project.

On March 7, 1942, the U.S. Army took over 4,725 acres of Los Angeles's holdings and established a World War II Japanese Relocation Camp. The first of 10,000 evacuees arrived March 25, 1942, and by that summer Manzanar was the biggest "city" between Reno and Los Angeles. Manzanar ("apple orchard" in Spanish) consisted of one square mile, fenced with barbed wire, with guard towers, barracks, mess halls, schools, and supporting structures. All that remains are the gatehouses, topped pagoda style, the old high school gym which is now a road maintenance station, and a white obelisk memorial to the dead.

Inyo 66. Los Angeles aqueduct.

Inyo 62-58. Fault scarp of 1872 earthquake, west of the highway.

Inyo 58. Graves of 1872 earthquake victims.

LONE PINE EARTHQUAKE OF 1872—At 2:30 a.m. on April 6, 1872, probably the largest earthquake in California's recorded history occurred near Lone Pine. The 8.3 magnitude quake killed 23, destroyed 52 of Lone Pine's 59 adobe buildings, triggered huge rockfalls in Yosemite, shook most of the western states, and rattled Salt Lake City. Movement along a fault zone extending from Big Pine to Olancha, a distance of some 60 miles, was in the order of six to ten feet in the Lone Pine area. This is typical basin and range faulting where the mountains continue to rise relative to the valleys.

A number of older fault scarps, some up to 20 feet in height, between Olancha and Bishop attest to the severe seismic activity in the Owens Valley in the past 10,000 years.

Inyo 58-56. **LONE PINE**—Pop. 1,684 (1980), El. 3,700'. Name derived from a tall Jeffrey pine tree growing at the confluence of Lone Pine and Tuttle creeks when the first settlers arrived in the Owens Valley in 1861. The pine tree was later washed out by flood but the name remained as the developing mines brought Lone Pine a floating population of many nationalities including Mexican, Welsh and Cornish.

Inyo 55. Traveler's Visitor Center—Good selection of publications covering the general area. Junction to Death Valley. *Rest Area.*

Inyo 54. Diaz Lake—Natural lake formed in a sink created by the 1872 earthquake. Named after Rafael and Eleuterio Diaz, brothers who had a cattle ranch on land surrounding the future lake in 1860.

Inyo 51-37. **OWENS LAKE**—Originally a large shallow alkaline lake which received the water of Owens River. Named by Fremont after Richard Owens, a member of his third expedition in 1845.

In the 1870s during activity of the mines at Cerro Gordo, small steamers carried ore from Swansea at the north end to Cartago at the south end of the lake. Owens Lake waters contained salt, soda and borax and in 1885, salt and soda processing plants were constructed providing a substantial part of the United States demand. In 1891, the lake was about 15 miles long, north to south, nine miles wide and 50 feet deep.

In 1907, Los Angeles started drawing Owens Lake water for use in southern California, and the lake was essentially drained by the 1920s.

CERRO GORDO—Silver and lead were discovered on the top of the Inyo Mountains northeast of Owens Lake by three Mexican prospectors in 1865. Named Cerro Gordo (Big or Fat Hill), it had bonanza ore worth $200 a ton; $17 million was produced making Cerro Gordo one of the great silver-lead districts in California.

Serious mining began in 1869, and in its peak year, 1874, 2,000 people resided in Cerro Gordo and three smelters poured out 5,300 tons of bullion worth $2 million. By 1877 the known deposits were worked out and small deposits were worked on and off until 1911 when new ore bodies of silver-lead and zinc were discovered.

The Cerro Gordo Freighting Company was organized in 1873 and operated 56 wagon teams until 1881. Ore was hauled from the mountain top by wagon to Keeler and Swansea along the east shore of Owens Lake, smelted, and the bullion then transported across Owens Lake by steamer to Cartago. Stations, watering places and camps were established and maintained along the Los Angeles route, requiring 21 days for a round trip. From Los Angeles, bullion was transported by rail to San Pedro and boated to San Francisco. Supplies to operate the mines were hauled in the opposite direction. The Cerro Gordo mines opened up the Owens Valley and transportation routes were developed connecting to Nevada and Los Angeles.

Inyo 52-21. The highway cuts across a series of alluvial fans forming from the mouths of canyons draining the Sierra.

Inyo 44. Cottonwood Charcoal Kiln cutoff (one mile east of highway) The kilns were used in the late 1800s to make charcoal used in the nearby mining districts of Cerro Gordo and Darwin (east of Owens Lake).

Inyo 37. Cartago—Pop. 75, El. 3,638'. Originally called Lakeville and Daneresburg by John Baptiste Daneri, native of Sardinia and a Lone Pine merchant, in the hope that he was creating "the Carthage of the West." Cartago was created as a steamer landing on the southwest shore of Owens Lake to handle shipments of silver bullion from Cerro Gordo.

Inyo 35. Olancha—Pop. 100, El. 3,650'. Named after an Indian tribe or village (Olanches).

Inyo 34. Early Olancha mill site. Junction to Death Valley.

Inyo 31. Los Angeles aqueduct.

Inyo 21. Pumice mine east of highway.

Inyo 18. *Rest stop.*

Inyo 15-5. **LITTLE LAKE VOLCANIC FIELD**—Made up of some 20 cones and related basalt flows, mostly east of the highway. Similar in age and origin to the Big Pine Volcanic Field. Note the low elliptical mounds (pressure mounds) caused by buckling of the upper cooled crust due to the movement of liquid lava beneath.

Inyo 10. Little Lake. Commercial resort and fish ponds. Originally Little Owens Lake, its springs have been a stopping place for travelers, prospectors, stages and freight teams for more than a hundred years. Just north of Little Lake are archaeological digs yielding artifacts indicating the presence of Indians during the past 5,000 years.

Inyo 10-5. The highway follows adjacent to a basalt flow originating from the Little Lake Volcanic field.

Inyo 1. Pearsonville—El. 2,470'.

Kern 29 (Kern 64). Junction U.S. 395 and California State 14. The Travel Guide follows California State 14. *Note change in mile markers.*

Kern 54. Small gold processing plant.

Kern 52. Indian Wells—An important early camp site used by the Jayhawkers party in January 1850 after crossing Death Valley.

Kern 41-38. **RED ROCK CANYON**—State Park. Series of tilted multi-colored Tertiary lakebeds, consisting of sandstones, mudstones, tuffs, overlying bleached and altered Tertiary volcanics.

Kern 36. **GARLOCK FAULT**—Major active northeast trending

fault that is related to, and joins with, the San Andreas fault to the southwest. An estimated 40 miles of horizontal movement and thousands of feet of vertical movement have occurred. This marks the approximate northwest boundary of the Mojave Desert.

MOJAVE DESERT—Vast area covering southeastern California, western Arizona and southern Nevada, with an average rainfall of less than four inches a year. Includes mountains of volcanics, granitic, sedimentary and metamorphic rocks, and valleys of Tertiary lake beds, alluvium and scattered volcanic fields similar to those found near Big Pine and Little Lake.

The Joshua tree is found only in the Mojave Desert region.

Kern 18. Experimental electric power generating windmills to west.

Kern 16. **MOJAVE**—Pop. 2,886 (1980), El. 2,756ʹ. Established August 8, 1876 as a Southern Pacific station, and probably named after the Mohave Indian tribe who inhabited the region. Junction of the Southern Pacific and Atcheson, Topeka and Santa Fe railroads. Terminus of the old Borax Road from Furnace Creek in Death Valley. Home of Voyager, which flew around the world without refueling in December 1986.

TWENTY-MULE TEAMS—1883-1888. Death Valley borax deposits were developed at Harmony and mining began in 1883. To reach the railhead at Mojave, twenty-mule teams were hitched to huge borax wagons with a payload of over 20 tons. The teams were handled by two men and pulled two large high-wheeled borax wagons and a water tank wagon, averaging about 15 to 20 miles a day. The round trip usually took a little more than three weeks, and 2.5 million pounds of borax were hauled from Death Valley each year. Operations lasted only five years when the Harmony Borax Works permanently closed down. "Twenty-mule team" remains a Borax trademark to this day.

Kern 14. Start Antelope Valley Freeway.

Kern 14-10. Mojave Mining District—Gold and silver discovered in 1894. Production approximately $15-20 million. Shell Oil Company mined gold from a small open pit from 1986-1988 at Mile Marker Kern 13.

Kern 4. Rosamond—Pop. 2,869 (1980), El. 2,415′. Established in 1888 as a Southern Pacific Railroad station. Named after the daughter of a railroad official, Rosamond is the gateway to Edwards Air Force Base.

(U.S. Borax Collection)

Twenty-mule teams hauled borax from Death Valley to Mojave between 1883 and 1889.

EDWARDS AIR FORCE BASE—Located 15 miles east of Rosamond adjacent to Rogers Dry Lake. Established in 1933 as Muroc Field covering 301,000 acres, the base was operated by the Army Air Force during World War II to develop supersonic jet and rocket aircraft. The X-1, flown by Chuck Yeager, broke the sound barrier (Mach 1.05), on October 14, 1947.

In 1947, the National Security Act turned the Army Air Force into the U.S. Air Force. In 1950 Muroc Army Air Base was renamed Edwards Air Force Base, after test pilot Glenn

Edwards, who died during a test flight of the Flying Wing.

On November 20, 1953, Scott Crossfield flew the D-558-2 to a record Mach 2. Three weeks later, Yeager flew the X-14 to Mach 2.4.

In the fall of 1958, the X-15 rolled out at Edwards and set speed and altitude records. In the mid-to-late 1960s the XB-70A and YF-12A were tested at Edwards.

In recent years, NASA Dryden Flight Research Center was added and Edwards has been used by NASA for space shuttle landings.

1960 NORTH AMERICAN X-15
Wing span—22'
Length—50'

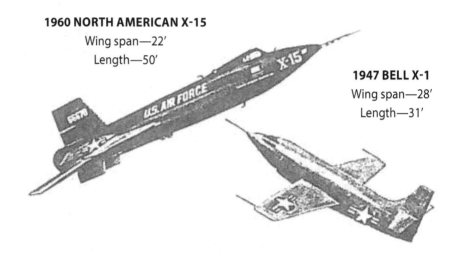

1947 BELL X-1
Wing span—28'
Length—31'

PANCHO BARNES—Just beyond Muroc Army Air Base was Pancho's Fly Inn, owned and operated by Pancho Barnes. Born Florence Leontine Lowe and raised in the affluent Los Angeles suburb of San Marino her first marriage was to the Rev. C. Rankin Barnes. In the 1920s, not accepting the position of a reverend's wife, she learned to fly and ran guns for Mexican revolutionaries, picking up the nickname Pancho.

In 1930 Pancho Barnes broke Amelia Earhart's air-speed record for women. Her flying experience and "go to hell" personality made her bar room a perfect after hours oasis for the hot shot flyboys in the late 1940s and 50s.

LA 71. **LANCASTER**—Pop. 48,027 (1980), El. 2,355'. Settled in 1877 by farmers from Lancaster, Pennsylvania.

LA 61-59. **PALMDALE**—Pop. 40,000, El. 2,655'. Settled in 1886 by

German Lutherans, it was originally called Palmenthal after the Joshua tree (Yucca palm). Town established June 7,1888, and name changed to Palmdale on August 13, 1890. Home of the B-1 Bomber.

LA 58-57. (Avenue S) **SAN ANDREAS FAULT**—One of the world's great active faults, it separates the Pacific sea floor plate on the west from the North American continental plate on the east. The Pacific plate is moving north-northwest, relative to the North American plate at an average rate of two to three inches per year. Movement in the last 25 to 30 million years is estimated to be 300 to possibly as much as 650 miles. Major earthquakes along the San Andreas fault include the Tejon Pass quake of 1857, magnitude 8+, and the San Francisco quake of 1906, magnitude 8.3. It is predicted that the southern California segment of the San Andreas Fault is due for a major earthquake of magnitude of 7 to 8+ sometime within the next 25 years.

Note crushed and contorted rocks in the road cuts. Also note the housing developments adjacent to and within the fault rift zone.

LA 57. California aqueduct—Brings water 440 miles from Tracy near the Sacramento delta in the San Joaquin Valley south through Bakersfield and to Perris in Riverside County.

West of the San Andreas Fault we enter the Pacific sea floor crustal plate. State 14 follows along the northern edge of the San Gabriel Mountains.

SAN GABRIEL MOUNTAINS—Part of the east-west trending transverse range of mountains found west of the San Andreas Fault. South of the highway the San Gabriel mountains consist of granites and metamorphic rocks.

LA 45. Escondito Summit—El. 3,258'. The highway cuts through a series of Tertiary marine sediments including shales, sandstones, conglomerates, and occasional volcanic flows.

LA 41. Vasquez Rocks—Series of tilted Tertiary sediments derived from the granites and metamorphic rocks of the San Gabriel Mountains, consisting of arkosic sandstones, breccias, and basalt flows. The area has been used for many years as a setting for western movies and TV shows.

LA 28. Placerita Canyon—Placer gold was discovered by Spaniards in 1842.

LA 28-26. Placerita Oil Fields—operated by Standard Oil and Getty Oil. First drilled and developed in 1875, and was the first commercial oil refinery in California.

LA 25. Junction of California State 14 and 1-5. Enter the San Fernando Valley. *Note change in mile markers.*

1-5 44. Terminus of Los Angeles aqueduct.

1-5 46. Sylmar—Site of February 9, 1971 earthquake (magnitude 5.6) with movement along a reverse fault along the southern edge of the San Gabriel Mountains. The Van Norman reservoir, south of the highway and now drained, almost breached during the shake.

1-5 49. **SAN FERNANDO**—Pop. 17,731 (1980), El. 1,021'. Mission San Fernando established in 1797 in St. Catherine of Bologua's Valley of the Live Oaks near four springs. Now known as the San Fernando Valley. City of San Fernando established in 1874.

1-5 58. **BURBANK**—Pop. 84,625 (1980), El. 622'. City laid out in 1887 on the Providencia Rancho and named for one of the subdividers, Dr. David Burbank, a Los Angeles dentist. Incorporated July 8, 1911 with 400 residents. Located in Burbank are the Lockheed Air Terminal and the Warner Brothers Studios.

1-5 62. **GLENDALE**—Pop. 139,060 (1980). El. 430'. Incorporated 1906. Originally named Riverdale, the name was refused by the Post Office Department in 1886 because another Riverdale existed near Fresno. Renamed Glendale (narrow valley) because of its location in the Verdugo Hills.
　　The site of Glendale was part of a 30,000 acre land grant given by the King of Spain to the Verdugo family in 1784, and operated for many years as a huge ranch.
　　The Cahuenga Capitulation Treaty, which ended Mexican California's part in the Mexican War, was signed at the ranch on January 13, 1847.
　　Only 13 American families lived on the site when the Southern Pacific Railroad reached Glendale in 1883.

26

1-5   71.   **LOS   ANGELES**—Pop.   2,968,579.   Consolidated metropolitan area, 11,497,568 (1980). El. 320'. Inhabited by the Shoshone Indians during the middle 1500s, Los Angeles was founded by the Spanish governor of Upper California on September 4, 1781. A party of 44 men, women and children of mixed nationalities and races settled along the Los Angeles River at a site near Union Station. Originally named the Town of Our Lady, Queen of the Angles of Porciuncula, this was a stopping point halfway between the San Gabriel and San Fernando Missions.

Mexico won its independence from Spain in 1821 and took over the government of Los Angeles in 1835 (the first part of the name was dropped), and Los Angeles developed into a rich farming community.

American troops captured Los Angeles during the Mexican War in 1847 and Mexico gave up the California region in 1848 after the war. Los Angeles was incorporated as an American city on April 4, 1850, five months before California joined the Union.

Los Angeles (pop. 1,610) was a sleepy village of mud huts surrounded by extensive ranchos, without a public school, newspaper or library. With its hot, waterless, dusty near-desert climate, its main activity was fighting Paiute Indians that raided the ranchos, driving off as many as 500 head of cattle. Two-thirds of the population was illiterate and the one-third literate were petitioning Congress to separate southern California as a state to be called Central California.

In 1851, as a result of the great gold rush which brought thousands to the area from around the world, law and order was a severe problem. On July 13, 1851, one day after the first southern California police force was organized, the mayor and council of Los Angeles organized a Vigilance Committee to handle the backwash of gold rush murderers, horse thieves, and highwaymen flocking to Los Angeles from the gold country. Subsequent records showed 40 "legal" hangings and 37 impromptu lynchings.

In 1861, southern California was still an unbroken cattle range and Los Angeles, with a population of 4,400, was having a hard time getting started. No government in Los Angeles was able to function. Assessed valuation of the city was $2 million and not one penny in taxes was collected. There was no valid reason to migrate to southern California. The first shade trees were only now being planted in Los Angeles.

In 1865, the Civil War ended and 2,000 people from the

ravaged South flocked to southern California because of cheap land (due to three years of drought) and also because of the similarity of climate. Real estate boomed and subdividing became big business. Tracts of land were bought by European emigrants resulting in ethnic communities.

Los Angeles realized that its future lay in a connecting railroad line to San Francisco, and in 1870 (Los Angeles, pop. 8,728), the Southern Pacific Railroad began construction of a line from San Francisco. The powerful Southern Pacific demanded and received the equivalent of enormous ransom to bring the line to Los Angeles, which was completed on December 6, 1876.

The Southern Pacific demanded the right to inspect the books of all companies using the line to ship freight and then fixed the freight rate at the point which would absorb all the profit. If a number of companies went bankrupt the Southern Pacific lowered the rates and when a company showed an increased profit, the rate was raised at once.

In 1873, southern California was still having problems. Industries included citrus (oranges and lemons), grapes for wine, and cotton. There were millions of acres of fertile land surrounding Los Angeles without water. No one wanted this acreage at any price.

Silver was discovered at Cerro Gordo, 150 miles north-northeast of Los Angeles and east of Owens Lake, in 1874. Silver lead ingots were shipped by wagon to Los Angeles and then to San Pedro. The population jumped from 11,000 in 1874 to 16,000 in 1875.

Because of drought, the depletion of Cerro Gordo ore, and small pox, the population of Los Angeles dropped back to 11,000 by 1880.

By 1885, developers in Los Angeles were already building ahead of demand, relying upon long-term exclusive franchises from government or the railroad companies to minimize their risks.

And so Los Angeles expanded, despite the absence of adequate schools or a host of other municipal services: a coastal city without a port, its growth fed by advertising, its development founded on the prospects of the future.

By 1887, the Santa Fe Railroad finally reached Los Angeles after an enormous two decade struggle with the Southern Pacific. A passenger fare war ensued whereby fares of $100 per passenger from Kansas City to Los Angeles were cut to $8 by the Santa Fe

Railroad on March 6, 1887, and then to $1 by the Southern Pacific Railroad on the same day. Thousands of easterners with dreams flocked west, resulting in a massive land-boom in southern California, and paper profits of $100 million by the end of 1887. The new towns of Glendale, Burbank, Azusa, Monrovia, Arcadia, Claremont, Cucaumonga and Colten were formed.

The southern California boom of 1887 brought the population to more than 100,000 and fizzled by the spring of 1888. Many miles of local railroad tracks eastward through the San Gabriel Valley, northward through the San Fernando Valley and westward to Santa Monica and Long Beach resulted from the boom. The "sleepy little town dozing in the sun" was finally on its way to becoming a major population center.

In the late 1890s, Los Angeles and San Francisco set out simultaneously to develop distant watersheds in a race that would ultimately go a long way toward determining which city enjoyed supremacy among the commercial centers of the Pacific Coast.

Steps taken by Los Angeles to develop Owens Valley water sources in the early 1900s led to large land speculation dealings. Upon delivery of the water in 1913, much of present day City of Los Angeles land was annexed, including most of the San Fernando Valley between 1914 and 1923.

Most of the San Fernando Valley land area was used for ranching and farming until after World War II. Rapid post-war growth has almost completely filled the San Fernando Valley with subdivisions.

Today, Los Angeles ranks as one of the largest cities in the world and certainly one of the most progressive.

La Ciudad de Los Angeles, early 1800s.

GEOLOGY

Geological processes which have shaped the western United States have just begun to be understood in the last 20 years. Major features, such as the Sierra Nevada and the Basin and Range Province, are directly related to plate tectonics, i.e., the movement and collision of crustal plates.

The collision between the North American continental plate and the Pacific sea floor plate occurred some 20 million years ago, and continues today as evidenced by periodic movement along the San Andreas fault. Related uplift, faulting and volcanic activity is also occurring in the western United States and will continue well into the future. Smaller-scale surface features, such as alluvial deposits and lakes, are generally the result of a combination of geologic processes (faulting, erosion, etc.), and climatic changes.

In the last one million years there have been four glacial periods separated by interglacial periods (each cycle approximately 20,000 years in length), which have affected the western United States. Evidence of glaciers can be seen along U.S. 395 between Bridgeport and Bishop. At present we are near the midpoint of an interglacial period.

Volcanic activity from three million years to less than 500 years in age is seen between Mono Lake and Little Lake. Rhyolitic volcanism related to granitic intrusion occurs between Mono Lake and Mammoth Lakes. Cinder cone activity and basalt flows are related to deep basin and range faulting and can be seen near Big Pine and Little Lake.

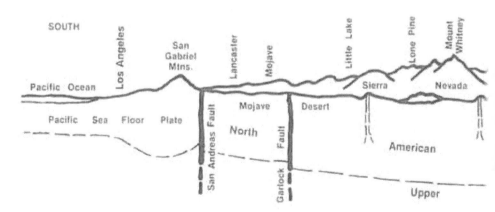

PRESENT DAY CRUSTAL CROSS SECTION ALONG

30

GLOSSARY

Batholith—A body of igneous rock that has intruded deep into the earth's crust and later exposed by erosion an area greater than 40 square miles. Called a **stock** if less than 40 square miles.

Caldera—A large depression in the area of volcanic activity, formed by volcanic explosion or collapse as the magma chamber is emptied.

Crustal Plate—Pieces of the earth's crust capable of movement. Can be continental or oceanic. Many major geologic features, such as volcanos, earthquakes, and mountains result when crustal plates collide.

Fault—A break in the earth's crust, along which there is movement.

Geologic Time Scale—A geologic calendar using relative ages of events on which an absolute time has been superimposed using radioactive decay of isotopes found in certain minerals.

Granite—A plutonic rock rich in quartz and potassium feldspar.

Igneous Rocks—Rocks formed by the crystallization of magma (molten rock below the earth's surface) or lava from volcanism.

Mantle—That part of the earth found between the core and the crust; approximately 1,800 miles in thickness.

Metamorphic Rocks—Rocks formed from pre-existing rocks through heat and/or pressure.

Orogeny—The process of mountain building.

Sedimentary Rocks—Layered rocks formed by the accumulation and solidification of sediments, or by chemical precipitation.

Subduction—The process by which a part of a crustal plate is forced down and under another crustal plate.

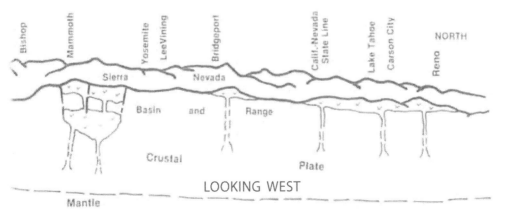

LOOKING WEST

U.S. 395, CALIFORNIA STATE 14 AND INTERSTATE-5.

GEOLOGIC CROSS SECTIONS

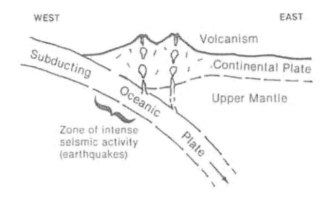

SIERRA NEVADA PLATE TECTONICS
125 - 80 Million Years Ago

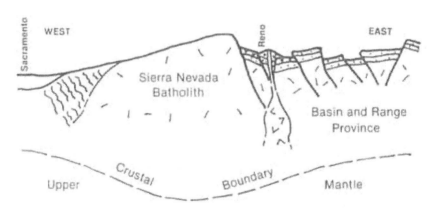

**PRESENT DAY CROSS SECTION SHOWING THE SIERRA NEVADA
AND THE BASIN AND RANGE PROVINCE**

GEOLOGIC TIME SCALE

ERA	PERIOD	EPOCH	ESTIMATED AGE (Millions Years Ago)	DOMINANT LIFE FORMS
Cenozoic	Quaternary	Recent	0.01	Animals and plants of modern types
		Pleistocene	1.6	
	Tertiary	Pliocene	5	Age of mammals and flowering plants
		Miocene	24	
		Oligocene	37	
		Eocene	58	
		Paleocene	66	
Mesozoic	Cretaceous		144	Age of reptiles, first birds, mammals, and modern fishes
	Jurassic		208	
	Triassic		245	
Paleozoic	Permian		286	Age of amphibians
	Pennsylvanian	Carboniferous		Conifers
	Mississippian		360	Modern insects
	Devonian		408	Age of fishes
	Silurian		438	Shells dominant
	Ordovician		505	First vertebrates & insects
	Cambrian		570	Invertebrates dominant
Precambrian				First invertebrates and plants

HISTORICAL CHRONOLOGY

10,000+ years. Indian presence in western United States.

1519-1821 Western United States claimed by Spain. Called Alta California.

1541-42 Coronado expedition into southwest United States.

1771 Mission San Gabriel built.

1821 Mexico wins independence from Spain and claims most of present day western United States.

1826 Jedediah Smith is first white man to cross present day Olvera Street in Los Angeles.

1841 Bidwell-Bartleson Party is first overland emigrant party to cross Nevada.

1843 First John C. Fremont expedition, with Kit Carson, explored Great Basin and Sierra.

1846 June 15. California breaks away from Mexico and raises United States flag.

1848 January 24. Gold discovered at Sutter's Mill. United States acquires present day Nevada from Mexico at end of the Mexican War.

1849 California Gold Rush. Placer gold discovered near Dayton, Nevada, which would lead to discovery of the Comstock Lode within 10 years.

1849-50 Brier Party of emigrants tragically wanders into Death Valley.

1850 September 9. California admitted as 31st state.

1851 Los Angeles incorporated as a city.

1859 Comstock Lode discovered and developed in Nevada.

1860 April 3. Pony Express began carrying mail between Sacramento, California and St. Joseph, Missouri.

1861 March 2. Nevada Territory established from western Utah Territory as the result of the mining rush to the Comstock and Virginia City in Nevada. October 24. Telegraph lines link the western United States between Omaha, Nebraska and Virginia City, Nevada when they joined in Salt Lake City, Utah. October 25. Last day of Pony Express.

1869 May 10. Golden spike driven at Promontory Point, Utah, joining the Central Pacific and Union Pacific railroads.

1870 Central Pacific Railroad changes name to Southern Pacific Railroad.

1872 Lone Pine earthquake—magnitude 8.3

1876 Southern Pacific Railroad completed between San Francisco and Los Angeles.

1876 Southern Pacific Railroad constructed from Los Angeles into Mojave Desert.

1885 Santa Fe Railroad arrives in southern California.

1887 Land boom in southern California.

1889 San Pedro harbor construction begins.

1892 Promotion of idea to construct 235 mile gravity flow water canal from Owens Valley to Los Angeles.

1901 Pacific Electric Railway created by Harry Huntington. Within two years 42 cities were linked within 35 miles of Los Angeles.

1905 Aqueduct concept to bring Owens Valley water to Los Angeles approved by Los Angeles Water Commission. Los Angeles population 206,000. San Fernando Valley opened to development at Pacoima with passage of Los Angeles aqueduct bond.

1905-1913 Design and construction of Los Angeles aqueduct. Water to be stored in San Fernando Valley.

1913 Construction finished on Los Angeles aqueduct.

1914 San Pedro harbor completed. Panama Canal completed and opened.

1931 Gambling permitted in Nevada.

REFERENCES

Fiero, Bill: *Geology of the Great Basin*, Univ. of Nev. Press, 1986.

Kahrl, W. L: *Water and Power*, Univ. of Calif. Press, 1982.

Rinehart, C. Dean and Smith, Ward C.: *Earthquakes and Young Volcanoes Along the Eastern Sierra Nevada*, Genny Smith Books, Palo Alto, California, 1982.

Stone, Irving: *Men to Match My Mountains*, Berkley Books, N.Y., 1956.

Made in the USA
Las Vegas, NV
20 September 2021